MW01657040

Get That Girl a Cheeseburger

Eating Disorder Myths and Misnomers

HALEY SNYDER

Copyright © 2014 Haley Snyder

All rights reserved.

LCCN: 2014903808

ISBN: 1495976912
ISBN-13: 978-1495976919

DEDICATION

This book is dedicated to the people who have supported me and helped to keep me alive during the most misunderstood and difficult times of my life. Because of them, I have been able to build my life worth living.

CONTENTS

ACKNOWLEDGMENTS

I want to thank my therapists, doctors, eating disorder professionals and dietitians, as well as Chris, Samantha, Julie, Larry, Dave, Michaela, Bethany, Kristin, Michelle and all of those who wished to be kept anonymous. All of these people have helped in the creation of this book – either by supporting me, or by contributing their story to this project. Without them, this book would not exist – and neither would I.

INTRODUCTION

Here I am, writing this book. Surreal. My name is Haley, and I have had an eating disorder since I was 5 years old. I was officially diagnosed at the age of 13, which is why I wanted to write a book that helps people comprehend this misunderstood genre. I am an extrovert and very open about my struggle and recovery. I will expand on my story later on in the book.

I have been blessed with a passion to meet people where they are at, and validate the human struggle that each and every person faces. I cannot count the amount of times people have asked me how they should support someone who is struggling. I have met complete strangers in restaurants, airports, waiting rooms, coffee shops, department stores, and other random places who, after striking up a conversation, find that they can relate with my story. They either have an eating disorder, or know someone who does. Most times the person is closely related to, or connected with someone battling this killer disease, and they have questions... lots of them. I often get the same questions and end up giving very similar advice to support people. More often than not, I hear "I just wish there was a map or guide for the support persons."

My support people have been the heroes in my story. What they have been through is a lot of what I presume you are facing. There are so many questions, and often support people look around and exclaim "Where do I get the information that I need to do this? I'm lost!" These sentiments come from a place of love and of concern for the person affected, also from a place of helplessness that occurs as you watch your loved one battle a highly misunderstood disease. Other thoughts come well into the fight when all hope seems lost. At that point, the questions turn to, "What else am I supposed to do? I feel like I never do anything right, and they just aren't getting better!" Other common questions are "What is this *thing*? How do I talk to my loved one about this struggle? What am I *not* supposed to say?"

Let me tell you, my support system has asked all of these questions and more, and as the eating disordered person, sometimes I don't have the answers - or the strength to explain the answers. So I am writing this book for you, the support, the unsung heroes in the fight against an eating disorder, the exhausted, confused, frustrated, sometimes angry, and seemingly stranded people who refuse to let this disease kill their loved ones.

Let me clarify what this book is NOT. This book is not written by an authority on eating disorders or the people that support them. It is written by me – a woman who grew up with an eating disorder, continues to devote her life to recovery, and who has had a lot of support. This book is also not an all-encompassing, heavily researched, academic book. My goal is to touch your heart rather than fill your head.

This project came about because I looked around and realized that most people really have no idea what eating disorders are all about, let alone how to support someone who is fighting to recover from one. This book is not meant to be a catch-all 'bible' of sorts for support people. It is purely an attempt to help you understand a little more about the situation that you are facing.

I pray that whatever you are going through, whoever you are dealing with, and however long you have been fighting, that you will find within these pages, a nugget of hope, a little direction, and hopefully some peace. Those of us with eating disorders are the ones fighting, and at the end of the day, our recovery is our responsibility. The blessing in that fact is that we, the eating disordered, have some control over how the story ends. Unfortunately, sometimes for you, it feels like you have no control over the outcome. This book has tools that you can use to understand the eating disorder, communicate with your loved one, and care for yourself. It may also be helpful to read this with a pen or highlighter in hand. Feel free to take notes and discuss with your loved one/support.

Please believe that you are not invisible, your job is very hard, and that is an understatement.... And it is worth it – I promise.

PART ONE

Welcome to the World of Eating Disorders.

1 SAY WHAT??

The lingo used in the world of eating disorders can be tricky and sometimes confusing. Throughout this book, and on your journey as a patient or supporter, there will be terms and abbreviations that you will be unfamiliar with. This chapter contains the most commonly used terms and phrases along with descriptions and definitions to help you obtain a better grasp on what you may read or hear.

ED – Acronym for Eating Disorder, also short hand personalization for the eating disorder. The 'empty chair technique' is a tool in the Gestalt school of psychology. It is intended to guide patients into a better understanding of themselves by imagining a part of themselves in a chair in front of them, separating themselves from the trait or quality that they wish to address. Often it is helpful for patients to separate themselves from their eating disorder in order to heal from the abuse it inflicts on their mind and body. In this technique, patients refer to their eating disorder by a name other than their own in order to separate the behavior from themselves as a person. As an example, a patient might refer to their eating disorder by saying "Geez, Ed is really harping on me today and making treatment very difficult". Other variations exist for this concept.

- Anna – Short hand personalization for Anorexia
- Mia – Short hand personalization for Bulimia

Symptom/Behavior - the use of a maladaptive coping mechanism (i.e.: restricting, bingeing, purging, compulsive exercise, cutting, abuse of weight loss pills, etc.)

Trigger – Something in the environment around a patient that incites an emotional or physical reaction. (i.e.: Often times, when a patient is coming out of treatment, family members will say "Oh honey, you look so healthy" which can trigger thoughts and feelings in the patient such as, "Healthy = Fat, I need to take action to prevent this from happening")

- **Thinspiration** – a culture of pro-anorexia and pro-bulimia websites, photos, and social media which glorifies excessive dieting, use of symptoms, and the desire to be underweight.

Restrict – reduce caloric intake by self-starvation.

Purge – artificial elimination of food via induced vomiting, laxative use, enema abuse, excessive exercise, etc.

Binge – consuming unusually large amounts of food, often in private.

Meal Plan – A prescription of the amount of food expected to be consumed by a patient per day. Treatment for an eating disorder almost always includes the input of a dietitian who, after working with the patient, will devise a daily blueprint for caloric intake – this is then turned into a meal plan. The patient follows the meal plan in order to regain their health and wellbeing while being monitored by the medical staff.

Tally/Exchange – The unit of measurement on a meal plan (i.e.: A patient may be prescribed 6 bread tallies in a day)

Re-feeding – The process of nourishing the body once again after an extensive use of symptoms, mainly regarding restriction. This process is very difficult on the patient physically, emotionally, and mentally and is often the first hurdle in healing from an eating disorder. (Please note: This is to be done by medical professionals as there are complications that can occur when not monitored closely.)

Recovery – The Holy Grail in the fight against an eating disorder. There are a lot of definitions of recovery, and they change with every author. My definition is that recovery is not static. I look at recovery as a journey away from an eating disorder, toward a life worth living. Recovery is not a destination where the eating disorder is gone and there are never struggles again (though this may be possible)... rather, I see it as a life where the eating disorder is present, but not in control. It is a state of skillful living in which the eating disorder is not active, and the person is living a joy-filled, effective life without needing symptoms to cope.

Self-Care – Self-care is anything a person does to nurture their mind, body, and spirit. This is an integral part of recovering from an eating disorder, and often seems counterproductive to the affected person. Examples of self-care include naps, social activities, massages, pedicures, playing games, visiting with family and friends, and anything else that supplements a healthy life.

Types of Eating Disorders

AN – Anorexia Nervosa

- An eating disorder in which the patient fails to maintain a body weight of at least 85% of what is expected for their age, height, and build. This disorder is also characterized by caloric restriction, a preoccupation with losing weight, and an intense fear of becoming 'fat'. Severely distorted body image is also a marker for the disease.

- It is estimated that 5-20% of people with anorexia will die from the disease, though when caught in time, treatment is very effective in the resolution of the disorder.

BN – Bulimia Nervosa

- An eating disorder in which the patient consumes large amounts of food (bingeing), and then eliminates (purges) the food through vomiting, abuse of laxatives, use of excessive or compulsive exercise, and/or periods of restriction.
- This disorder can be deadly and can severely damage the gastro-intestinal system, ruin teeth, and lead to heart attack and strokes.
- Prognosis is good once acknowledged and treated. People with bulimia tend to accept treatment more readily due to the fact that the symptoms are more obvious and it is hard to deny that there is a problem.

BED - Binge Eating Disorder

- An eating disorder characterized by the consumption of unusually large amounts of food. The behavior is often done in secret and is a cause of shame for the disordered individuals.

- While this disorder is serious and dangerous, treatment has proven especially helpful in the resolution of the disease.

EDNOS – Eating Disorder Not Otherwise Specified

- The is very specific regarding diagnosis of eating disorders. When patients do not fully meet the exact symptoms of Anorexia, Bulimia, or Binge Eating Disorder, they are diagnosed with EDNOS.
- According to the National Alliance on Mental Illness (NAMI), approximately 75% of diagnosed eating disorders fall under this category.
- It is important to note that EDNOS is just as harmful and deadly as Anorexia, Bulimia, and BED. The only difference is that the symptoms may be atypical or slightly varied from a traditional eating disorder diagnosis.

- EDNOS is different for every individual. The symptoms can be a mixture of any defined eating disorder. One person may restrict and purge whatever they do eat, while another may binge then over exercise and follow that with a week of restriction. Just because someone's eating disorder doesn't fit perfectly within the criteria for AN, BN, or BED does not mean that they don't have an eating disorder. It means that they have EDNOS.

Note on Diagnosis: This and other diagnosis have changed some with the development of the DSM-V which has just recently been released and is not in general use at this point.

Co-Occurring Disorders – Many times, when someone is diagnosed with an eating disorder, they are also diagnosed with other disorders such as depression and anxiety. Patients can also suffer from PTSD, bipolar disorder, borderline personality disorder, schizophrenia, among others. While not all eating disordered patients have co-occurring disorders, for those that do, the care team must make important decisions regarding the type of treatment that they administer.

Another important area that is often addressed in the diagnosis and treatment of eating disorders is chemical dependency. It is not unheard of for people with eating disorders to have addictions to drugs or alcohol. There are many programs that address both issues in tandem.

People Involved:

Patient – the person struggling with an eating disorder. This is not to say that the person IS the eating disorder, rather, it is a battle that they fight daily with the help of support persons and care teams. The patient is the person who is building a life worth living every time they say no to the eating disorder.

Support Person – The brave soul that encourages consistent movement toward recovery, is a shoulder for the patient when nothing seems to be going right, and the resilient person who consistently cares about the health and wellbeing of the patient. The support person is also who encourages healthy behaviors, and often finds themselves frustrated, but pushes on anyway knowing that this struggle is life threatening. These people are committed to holding up their loved one during the fight against an eating disorder.

Care/Treatment Team – A group of professionals that help a patient recover from an eating disorder and heal from issues that plague the individual. Often consists of a psychiatrist, psychologist, medical doctor, dietitian, and care manager. This team can also include occupational therapists, physical therapists, chaplains, and other professionals committed to the health and wellbeing of the patient.

- **Psychiatrist** – The person who the patient sees for psychiatric evaluation and medication management. A psychiatrist is a certified medical doctor with a specialty in psychiatry. Appointments are often short and focused on the diagnostic and medical side of an issue.

- **Psychologist** – The psychologist is also known as the 'therapist' or 'counselor'. This person works with the patient on emotional issues that may be affecting the individual's ability to live a productive and fruitful life. Psychologists often work with the family of patients in order to set up a supportive environment at the patient's home. Appointments are often an hour long, and focus on the emotional, behavioral and relational issues associated with the treatment.

- **Medical Doctor** – In any treatment setting, the patient will be assigned a medical doctor that will monitor the physical wellbeing of the individual. Often this includes regular monitoring of blood pressure, pulse, labs, weight, and physical development.

- **Dietitian** – The licensed professional that works with the patient on nutritional needs and goals. This person will use the tools they have (such as meal plans, worksheets, and experiential teaching) in order to help the patient learn normal eating and eventually reintegrate into a normal life with a healthy appreciation of their individual nutritional needs.

- **Care Manager/Case Manager** – This person is the liaison between the patient and insurance. They work with the care team and coordinate treatment plans for the patient that will be adequately covered by insurance. They are the patient advocate.

- **Chaplain** – In some treatment settings, chaplains are available to meet with patients in order to address the eating disorder and other issues from a faith-based perspective. Most chaplains are trained in many religions in order to accommodate the majority of patients. Spirituality can be a very important part of recovery.

- **Occupational Therapist** - The professional that works with the patient on a multitude of areas such as body acceptance, daily living in recovery, grocery shopping, cooking, etc.

- **Physical Therapist** – Works with patients on strengthening their bodies while staying cognizant of the eating disorder. They are skilled in working with all body types and in this setting, have often specialized in mind and body treatments as well.

Treatment and Therapy Models

DBT – Dialectical Behavior Therapy

- This therapy was initially developed by Dr. Marsha Linehan, Professor of psychology at the University of Washington. This therapy consists of modules in which the patient learns distress tolerance, emotional regulation, interpersonal effectiveness, acceptance and mindfulness.
- This therapy is often used to help patients deal with frequent suicidal thoughts, impulsivity, and intense emotions which result in self-destructive behavior.

CBT – Cognitive Behavioral Therapy

- This therapy is based primarily on the theory that thoughts, feelings, and behaviors are interconnected. For instance, thoughts can lead to feelings which can then result in behaviors, or behaviors may provoke a feeling and it could lead to thoughts which perpetuates the problem.

- CBT works on a list of cognitive distortions, and helps patients to recognize and change ineffective or negative thinking patterns, and build new thought patterns that are more effective.

CBT-E – Cognitive Behavioral Therapy for Eating Disorders

- This therapy was devised at Oxford in response to the prevalence of relapse in the lives of eating disordered patients. This therapy is a very structured, prescriptive plan executed by the psychologist while working with the patient.
- Often this therapy takes no more than 20 weeks and consists of building an effective life outside of therapy by

changing behaviors and charting a new course with the help of the therapist.

- This therapy has shown a much better recovery rate from eating disorders than other therapies, though it doesn't fully address past issues or co-occurring disorders.

Inpatient treatment - This is an intensive treatment in which the patient stays at the hospital/treatment center with the goal of medical stabilization and symptom interruption. This is often a short term intervention, lasting one to four weeks. This treatment is used for patients who are medically unstable, or who are unable to cease using destructive eating disordered behaviors.

Intensive outpatient - This treatment is generally used when the patient is medically stable, but struggling with symptom use, or having difficulty living an effective life outside of treatment. This is also a common treatment used after release from an inpatient or residential program. It affords more support than outpatient, and helps the patient focus on life skills designed to create a life of recovery. The structure of these programs range dramatically, though the majority have programs lasting three to eight hours per day Monday through Friday.

Outpatient treatment – This measure is used when the patient is medically and psychologically stable, and able to cope with life effectively without using the eating disorder as a *primary* coping mechanism. Outpatient treatment can consist of weekly, bi-weekly, monthly, or quarterly appointments with the care team in order to maintain a healthy and productive life. Outpatient treatment supports the patient with skills and strategies to live in recovery.

Residential treatment – This option can be used when a patient is struggling with the eating disorder and is having difficulty maintaining a life of recovery. The stay ranges from three weeks up to nine months. Often patients have utilized inpatient, intensive outpatient, and/or outpatient before this option is discussed. There are many residential treatment facilities in the United States, and they prove to be helpful in the creation, practice, and maintenance of life skills needed to live a life free from an eating disorder.

Support Groups – Groups often facilitated by a trained professional in whom patients can share concerns and victories when working toward recovery. There are support groups for virtually every problem, eating disordered or otherwise. If there are not support groups at the treatment center your loved one attends, there may be some in the community.

2 MY STORY

I have struggled with an eating disorder since I was a young girl. I won't go into extreme details, because that is not the concern of this book, nor is it relevant to the way I was supported by family and friends. I will say however, that my eating disorder is a coping mechanism that I used to deal with the memories and side effects of multiple traumas that spanned the first 26 years of my life.

My specific eating disorder was fueled by the intense desire to disappear. There were a lot of challenges in my life early on including physical and sexual abuse. These events started a domino effect resulting in a change of caregivers and subsequently adjusting to a new family. As a little one, I learned to believe that I was a waste of space, worthless, and that I was a 'bad girl'. My world didn't seem safe, and I felt that I was alone. I lived in a hyper vigilant state of fear, and I wanted so badly to disappear. The only way I figured I could do that was to stop eating, though it wasn't a conscious decision. With all of the changes going on, it made a lot of sense that my parents didn't notice that something was wonky with my relationship to food. I lived with my dad and stepmom (who I would later call mom, and who also contributed to this book) from the time I was five. At 8 years old and after a couple of moves, we settled down in a small town west of Minneapolis, Minnesota.

By middle school, I was diving head first into a sea of insecurity, awkwardness, and shame due in part to some pretty intense bullying. According to the bullies, I was too fat, too weird, too... well, too 'everything negative' to consider including me in their group. Ninth grade rolled around and my friend asked me to try out for cheerleading with her. I was convinced that I wouldn't make the squad, but I figured I would try out and see what happened. After all, cheering with your best friend... dream job right? This was a new opportunity to make the bullying stop, I was excited.

I got on the team! That meant daily workouts, modified eating habits, excessive focus on body image, and an overwhelming expectation to be everything to everyone (as if I wasn't already a people pleaser).

The competitive nature of cheerleading was good for me, it pulled me out of my shell and out of my head and forced me to meet people and be social. It is true when they say that anything in excess is too much. This period in my life is when I learned how to over-achieve in every area of my life. Go big or go home, right?

I decided I was going to be the prettiest, thinnest, fittest, most volunteering, best singing, grade 'A' student that ever did grace the halls of Central High School. I was working out, cutting calories, studying late into the evening, going to every sporting event, volunteering for church, keeping my goody two shoes polished and sparkling, and making sure that everyone was happy – parents, siblings, friends, teachers, church members, coaches, etc. I was still insecure and unhappy, but at least I was being accepted.

I was about 4 months away from turning 14, and my new determination to perfect everything about myself was in full swing... until I stopped losing weight. We were in off-season training for cheerleading and my coaches brought my weight to my attention... they said I was too heavy and I was cutting corners in workouts. They shamed me in front of my team, and put restrictions on me with the promise that those restrictions would be lifted when more weight was lost. This ultimatum, having verified my own negative self-image and threatened that which I feared most, exclusion, caused a shift in me from determined to obsessed, from wanting to disappear to chasing perfection, and it showed in all areas of my life. I was about to become much more miserable.

In the spring of my freshman year, I went on a choir trip to Chicago and stayed in a hotel room with two senior girls. I thought they were so cool. I confided in them that I felt fat and didn't know what to do about it. I asked how they stayed so thin and they showed me the ropes. I started taking diet pills that week and I started to purge.

It was nearing the end of the school year, and the beginning of a new goal. I had decided that by the end of the summer, I would be in perfect shape and would blow my coaches out of the water with my athletic ability and stunning figure. I knew this would take a drastic change in my behavior, and I started using what I had learned - secretly purging whatever I ate. It worked and I lost weight; at the expense of my grades, my voice, my health, and my friends.

Then May 20th, 1999, happened. Mom and dad announced that we would be having family dinner at Hardee's and then watching a movie at the theater. I was terrified. *"How was I going to eat a full meal and keep it inside for 3 hours??"* I plotted about my food choice during the ride to the restaurant, deciding on a salad and a diet coke. To my dismay, they were out of salad. I lost my breath, forced myself to regroup and after a long, labored pause, I ended up settling on a grilled chicken sandwich. After dinner, I panicked and excused myself to the bathroom. Something tipped my parents off. My mom followed me and caught me standing backward in the stall facing the wall. She startled me, "*What are you doing?!*" My skin went ice cold and I tried to lie and tell her that I was unbuckling my belt. She called my bluff (I never was good at lying). I was purging. In the monotone voice of a parent struck with fear, she spoke: *"Finish up, meet me at the table."* I had never wanted to crawl into a hole so bad in my life. The anger in my parents' eyes was astonishing. I had never seen her or my dad so upset. They were so confused, concerned, and alarmed about my behavior, and angry that I had been lying to them.

Enter the beginning of the supporter and supported relationship.

Before I knew it, I was in outpatient therapy twice a week for the summer. (This was before treatment was well known.) The assumption that my family held, was that this was a phase, and something that self-centered teenage girls do. I don't remember anything about that stint in treatment except a patchwork quilt made of jeans that hung on the wall in the waiting room. It was covered in quotes like "size zero equals nothing", and "worth is not measured in pounds" written in puff paint.

By the end of the summer, I hadn't reached my goal of perfection but I was 'better' and I returned to school. Cheerleading, academics, and the normal grind of pleasing everyone (or attempting to do so) were my focus again. The only thing that differed was that I had a new understanding of what an eating disorder was, and how to hide my means of losing weight and my weight loss. I look back and feel really bad for all of the deception I created and all of the food that I threw away in the trashcan outside of my school.

During my high school years, my parents did what they could to help me 'get rid' of the eating disorder. They showed public displays of concern for sneaky behaviors, had people spy on me at school to see if I was eating what I ordered in the cafeteria, laid guilt trips about lying and suggested that I was being a bad role model for my little sister and brother, among other things.

I couldn't wait to go to college. I graduated high school and was accepted to a University three hours away from my parents. At first I was terrified. I stayed in my dorm room and cried for a solid three days. At some point in the middle of the third night,

I realized that this was my chance... I was 18 and no one knew or cared what I was doing regarding my food or gym habits. I took full advantage of the freedom.

This is the point in my life where I learned that 'commitment to health and fitness' was highly touted and a point of pride for many people. I was just as consumed as I was in high school, only I had more time on my hands, and a new kind of peer pressure to deal with. Now it wasn't only about being thin and accepted, it was also about being attractive to the guys on the other side of the quad, and envied by the girls in my dorm. I felt like if I wasn't on top of the pack, I was drowning. I felt that I needed to aim very high in order to be equal to those around me.

Three months went by. In that time, I had visited the dining hall about once a week and the gym seven times as much. I had also survived a rape, and a dose of the 'date-rape drug'. In November, I returned home for Thanksgiving. The expressions on people's faces were surprising to me. I didn't think that I had lost much weight; I thought I was just as fat and ugly as ever. I was blown away by my family's response. They were asking me not to lose any more weight. All of the negative attention not only confused me but made me angry. *"How dare they dismiss all of the work I had done to be 'healthy'?!"* I got defensive, rolled my eyes, avoided the holiday food, and went back to school. By December, I was passing out in the dorm hallways, finding myself lost - not knowing where I was supposed to be, terrified of everything and everyone, and generally miserable – but I was thin.

Over winter break, I floundered, not quite comfortable in my own surroundings. I was unable to cope with the drama at home; my parents were unhappy in their marriage, my sister and brother were feeling the heat, I was feeling judged, and everyone was putting food in front of me. Spring semester came and I was convinced that I gained all of the weight back over holiday vacation, so I made my 'new year's resolution' and continued on in the pursuit of perfection. By now, I had a group of friends who were just as committed to "health and fitness". It was easy to get back into the competitive dieting and drastic weight loss.

Just as I was getting used to the demands of the semester, and back into 'shape', I began my first romance. He thought I was hot. *"WHAT?? A guy thinks I am hot... and fun to hang around with?? He must be out of his mind."* He was my first love, and it lasted 2 weeks.

Lesson One in Dating: If he seems off balance, he probably is...

I managed to get over my first heart break and keep my slender figure through the spring semester. My grades had slipped tremendously due to the fog that blanketed my brain, and the classes that I missed while being passed out in various areas on campus. I was no longer a 4.0 student; my life was starting to crumble.

When summer came around, I decided to stay with my best friend and her family near the campus instead of returning home to the disapproving eyes of a family who didn't understand 'health'. I spent the summer at the beach, in church, and working both at a lingerie store and a shoe store in the mall. I felt terrible. The muscle aches, mood swings, low energy, dizziness, confusion, and short attention span plagued my days and haunted my nights.

School began again in September, and with that I was allowed access to the university workout facilities again – my sanctuary. I had no idea that I was tempting death every time I worked out and every time I got behind the wheel. At this point, my heart had weakened to a point that warranted inpatient hospitalization, and my liver was on the brink of shutting down. I thought I was healthy – I was the exact weight I 'should' be on the BMI graph, and I 'knew' that

I could still stand to lose 20 more pounds. I pressed on.

The holidays came around and I started dating my 'first love' again, this time it was 'for good', it was true love. December came and went marked only by the critical looks and hushed whispers from family and friends regarding my weight and newfound rapidly deepening relationship.

In January 2004, I ended up unconscious on the landing of a split level stairwell in the music department at the university. I remember students walking over me, bewildered and rushed; not quite knowing how to react or what to do. They paused, stared, and then hesitantly continued on to their next commitment. During a brief return to consciousness, I was able to get a text out to my best friend who lived near to campus. I told her that I thought I had the flu, and I knew I couldn't drive. I asked her for a ride (still in denial that there was a problem). An hour later, I was being rushed to the hospital by paramedics. They kept expressing their surprise that I was still alive as my blood pressure continued to drop. I thank God that my best friend came to my aid that day. She was the angel that I needed when I would have otherwise died on that landing.

Valentine's Day came and he asked me to marry him!! I said yes. He promised me the world, and we dreamed of future houses, babies, vacations, life. I dropped out of school due to my health, and while my new fiancé was praising my weight loss, my family was growing increasingly concerned and frustrated (rightfully so). My parents had separated at that point, and I had come down with a terrible case of mono which was only complicated by severe dehydration and malnutrition. I lay on my mom's couch and cried for weeks while she quietly made me scrambled eggs and supplied water to my needy body.

By April I was over the hump of mono, and I was fully consumed by an exercise addiction and anorexia (neither of which I was aware of). At this point, my fiancé had a change of heart and he and my parents begged me to go to treatment. In May I started a partial hospitalization program. I spent 8 hours a day learning how to eat again, going to therapy, seeing dietitians, being monitored by doctors, and practicing self-care. I was staying at my future in-laws with my fiancé during this time, and I began to rebuild my life.

A year later in July, I turned 20 and I had been symptom free for a whole year. I had restored weight and was eating a full meal plan, exercising responsibly, and living in my own apartment while attending cosmetology school.

The wedding was planned for the next summer, and I was sure that my future was going to be a 'happily ever after' story.

In November, my mom was battling breast cancer and my parents were ending the separation and getting a divorce. I began working for a large salon chain and had my eyes set on the ladder that I was intent on climbing. It was then that my fiancé started to change his attitude little by little. Hints started to come out of the woodwork. He was asking if we should work out together, suggesting leaner foods, offering to buy workout clothing and aerobic videos for me, and generally focusing on a 'healthy' lifestyle. I was madly in love, and figured if he saw a problem with my body; it must be a legitimate concern. After all, I had gained weight since we had met, and it made sense to me that this would be a shock for him. Another concern that he voiced was that 'Christian women' were to 'respect' their husbands and that by 'letting myself go', I was disrespecting him before the marriage even began. He threatened to leave if I didn't correct this problem before the wedding.

Seven months later, it was our wedding day and I had lost 60 pounds. I wasn't starving or over exercising, I was keeping it in balance, and was getting a LOT of positive attention from him and everyone else. People were amazed at my ability to have such self-control while simultaneously moving from stylist to manager in the salon, and planning an entire wedding.

A month before the wedding, my family started to show increased concern for me and my decision to get married. They knew that I was naïve, and they only wanted the best for me so they encouraged me to take an honest look at whether this was something I wanted to do. Naturally, I got offended and angry. When they started in on my weight loss, I blew up. *"All of you are either obese or divorced and in some cases – BOTH! How dare you tell me what to do with my life?? I am finally healthy and marrying the love of my life!"* I lashed out and pushed a lot of people away.

A week before the wedding, I sat down with my fiancé with the intention of relieving the dissonance that I felt between my family and my decisions. I addressed him honestly, *"Honey, I want to marry you, but before I walk down the aisle, I need you to know a couple of things. I want children, and I want to travel. Those are my only requirements. If you don't want those things, we need to walk away now."* He was offended that I even asked, but he coolly and diplomatically responded, *"Of course baby, there is nothing more intimate and sacred than making another human being together, and I want to see the world with you!"*

The day arrived, and to my surprise, everyone showed up for the wedding. My family was doing their best to support me even though they knew in their hearts that I was walking down a dangerous path. After we signed the marriage license and it was final, my stomach felt sick. A day later, we were at the airport getting ready to leave on our honeymoon. As we walked down the jet way, he leaned over and whispered to me, *"I hate this traveling shit, and we are not having kids."* I felt the jail doors slam shut and my life sentence officially begun.

For the next 4 years, I lived in hell. My husband had his own demons and dealt with them by controlling me. He counted my calories, watched me work out, weighed me daily, and was obsessed with all of my shortcomings. After all, he believed that the man was the head of the household and the woman was created to respect him. When I didn't fulfill his expectations, he punished me physically and emotionally, non-verbally reminding me of my status as 'less-than'. As I continued to lose weight, I also started losing the people around me. I was consumed with making him and my boss happy at the expense of my family and my health. I was working 60 hours per week, working out 2-4 hours a day, counting (and restricting) every calorie I consumed, all while maintaining my church attendance, attending family functions, volunteering, and putting him through college.

By this point I had relegated my family to a backseat (or trunk spot) in my life and they had become unhappy with who I was. They saw me as self-important, stuck up, and a pious woman. I was surrounded by people who didn't like me – I was essentially alone.

Three years after I was married, I had a nervous breakdown. I was at work and began to display stroke-like symptoms. I couldn't walk in a straight line, I was slurring my words and I was really confused about where I was and what I was doing. I had my husband pick me up from work. When he got there, he spent the 20 minute car ride to the hospital berating me for being out of shape and stressing about the fact that we were losing money while I was away from work. We saw the doctor, and they started running every test in the book.

After a week in the hospital and multiple medical consultations, it was clear that I was malnourished, severely dehydrated, suffering from PTSD, and chronically stressed beyond my limits. From this point, my life changed completely. At 25 years old, I was medically and mentally unstable, and did not have a safe place to go to outside of the hospital.

During my aftercare, a therapist suggested that I seek help at the eating disorder treatment center. Reluctantly, I went in for my initial assessment. After many tests and a long conversation, the doctor asked if I had my bags packed. I was confused until she told me that I was very sick and was being admitted to the inpatient unit to become medically stable. I was stunned. I told her I would go on one condition – that I wasn't the biggest woman on the unit. She assured me that was not the case.

Fourteen days later, I left the inpatient ward and started 6 weeks of intensive outpatient treatment; I had gained strength and had started to realize the gravity of the situation I was in. My dad had just remarried, my husband was growing increasingly anxious about the small amount of weight that I had gained, my mom and sister had almost written me off, and I was losing the career that I had worked so hard to create. I was also still enslaved by the obsessive thoughts and self-hatred that fuelled the eating disorder.

I started to confront my husband about his expectations, and around Christmas, I told him that he was doing nothing less than abusing me. At this juncture there were only 2 directions we could go... get better, or fall apart. In true abuser fashion, he begged, pleaded, and promised that he would be a better husband and assured me that he couldn't live without me. As an insecure woman terrified of failure and abandonment, I believed him. He then asked me to lose more weight because he wasn't at all attracted to me anymore.

In January, I was again medically unstable and hospitalized (admitted on the same day that my uncle died – I had to miss the funeral). Hubby was furious that I had gotten 'caught' for losing more weight. He became increasingly distant, and my family was doing their best to support me even though they sometimes didn't want to.

I was in the hospital for 6 more weeks, and was discharged on Valentine's Day. That day, my life was again permanently changed.

My husband asked for a divorce at 8:30am, before I had even gotten home from the hospital. We told the people around us that it was mutual and that we were better friends than spouses. I was stunned and grateful at the same time. I was heartbroken, and free, I didn't know what to think. I never went back to my own bed; I was sent to my mother's house. A few days later, he dropped off whatever material items he deemed were mine.

Over the next year, I found out from various people that he had been cheating on me for a long time. I was humiliated and torn apart. I used my eating disorder to cope with the pain. I bounced around in different levels of treatment, became intimate with one too many men, and had to face the fact that the very people I was living with acted as if they hated me. As supporters, they were exhausted and at a loss. There was no clear road to recovery and there were misconceptions both on mine and their part. We lacked the skills necessary to work together and we were forced to learn how to be a team in the fight against this disorder. It took a lot of talking, and yelling, and crying but we had to come to a place where we were all on the same page.

I came to accept what their views and assumptions were of me, and they learned what the truth was behind the façade and closed doors. They saw the face that was behind the mask, and I had to recognize and undo all that my ex-husband had created. In the end we found that he was lying not only to me, but was also actively dismantling my family all while I starved myself to make him happy.

I tell the story of my courtship, marriage, and divorce only to illustrate that he was the incarnation of my eating disorder. He is a perfect mirror of what an eating disorder does in the heads and lives of people who are affected. He fed on my insecurities and ripped my life to shreds with surgical precision.

The eating disorder destroys all relationships (especially those closest), it is drenched in lies, veiled in secrecy, controlling to an unimaginable degree, fueled by fear and feelings of inadequacy, and intent on isolating the person until they shrivel up and die: emotionally, spiritually, and eventually physically.

From the time I was diagnosed with an eating disorder at 13 years old, my family was there to support me in my recovery. Sometimes they hated it, and sometimes it hurt like hell. Sometimes it was rewarding for them, feeling like they were making headway. They also went through a myriad of emotions such as: frustration, fear bordering on terror, anguish, angst, rage, helplessness, hopelessness, self-blame, guilt and responsibility, sleeplessness, loss of appetite, depression and anxiety. They went through hell, they met me at the bottom, and they soared to the peaks with me.

Ultimately, it was up to me to seek out and work for recovery, but I wouldn't have lived without their love and encouragement. Throughout my entire story, my family was there, in the background. They weren't always effective, and they could have done a lot of things differently; AND they stuck with me when everyone else walked away. They fed the fire inside of me that said "I want to fight", they held me when I refused to be held, loved me when I couldn't love myself, and more than anything, they kept trying even when they had no clue what to do – taking stabs in the dark in an attempt to kill the very disorder that was trying to murder me.

Over the years, we have all learned the ins and outs of this eating disorder, and have learned a few key principles:

- The goal is progress, not perfection.
- Building a life worth living is the only way to extinguish a life worth hating.
- What you see on the outside rarely reflects what is happening on inside.
- Success is not the extinction of the eating disorder; it is the ability to live in this world without leaning on the eating disorder to cope.
- Walking in recovery can only be done one day at a time.
- Recovery is furthered by an intense honesty with oneself and the people who support you.

There is no perfect way to support someone with an eating disorder, there is no handbook. Half of the things you do will be counterproductive, and the other half might be shot down, but in the big picture, the consistency of the support is what will help your loved one recover from this deadly enemy. It is a life and death battle, but with support, it is possible for someone to recover and live a beautiful life they may have never imagined for themselves.

I owe my life and my recovery to my main support Jesus Christ. He is my Lord and my salvation, my rock and fortress, and He has been there holding my heart through every trauma, every tear soaked night, every terrifying meal, and every waking (and sleeping) moment of my life. He says He will bring beauty from my ashes and that He has a plan for my life. I know that I cannot change my past; I cannot erase the rape, or the abuse, or even regret my way out of a bad marriage. What I *can* do is pray fervently for every person and family who is being assaulted by eating disorders. I can use my love for writing to make a difference in the lives of those I am passionate about. I can trust that God will place my story in the right hands at the right time so that someone can get the help and encouragement that they so desperately need. I can continue living recovery every day in order to prove that it is, in fact, possible to have a life worth living.

I am not fully recovered, and some say that there is no day where 'recovered' happens. I am on the journey of recovery, and I struggle, sometimes daily. I have worked very hard to learn skills to deal with the thoughts and emotions that lead to eating disordered behavior, and I use those skills as often as possible. Relapses, lapses, and slip-ups occur, but the determination and strength that it takes to do the 'next right thing' is always available, if not within myself, in the eyes and hearts of my support.

Note:

While the actions of others were at minimum questionable, I take responsibility for allowing the people around me to dictate my actions and reactions. My core beliefs were that I wasn't good enough, and that I couldn't stand to be alone. As such, it was natural that I fell into the trap of changing for the people that I loved.

I will never know what would have happened had I taken a stand and said "this is NOT okay", and chosen to walk away. What I know now, however, is that I don't ever have to live under the oppression of my eating disorder or another human again.

There is a freedom that comes with recovery, and I pray that every person reading this book will find that freedom and run with it.

3 MY SUPPORTER'S STORIES

There were two people who have been the most involved in my illness and recovery. While there were many people around, these two have really taken the brunt of the supporter responsibility, both good and bad. These are their stories:

My Step-Mom:

When Haley was diagnosed with an eating disorder for the 3rd time, I first thought, "No big deal... we've been here before and it's always been short term, and then we move on."

This all started when my daughter was thirteen. I found her attempting to stick her finger down her throat to get rid of the food we had just eaten. This was at the end of a school year so we got her into treatment over the summer. As summer drew to a close, we discussed whether or not treatment would continue. Weighing heavily on the decision was whether or not she could be in treatment, plus be a cheerleader on the football team. At the time, she chose cheerleading. I thought we were 'done' with all treatment because in my mind, this was all about Haley being 'skinny' so she could fit in with her friends and the other cheerleaders. I also thought that she just needed something that she cared about more than being 'skinny' and since she made the choice to stick with cheerleading; I thought that would fill that void. Oh – I was so wrong!

Let's fast forward to her freshman year of college. Leaving Haley at the dorm was one of the most difficult things I've ever done in my life, but I had no idea how difficult things were actually going to get. Being 3 hours away, I was not seeing her on a regular basis though we talked frequently. What I didn't know is that she had relapsed and was not only restricting, she was exercising excessively as well. After 12-14 months, her body started shutting down. She ended up with a severe case of mono and spent a couple of weeks at my house so I could nurse her back to health. But she was far from healthy. Ultimately, she had to leave school to enter treatment again. At that time she was engaged to be married and even though I was helping and supporting her, I was also comforted by the thought that she had the support of her fiancé and his family as well. Again – I was so wrong!

By the time Haley's wedding came, she was doing very well in treatment and I was encouraged that she was making good choices regarding her health. She was working out regularly, but not excessively and she was eating healthy foods. What I didn't know – what no one knew – was that she was not making any of these choices herself. She was, in fact, being controlled and shamed by her husband.

It took several years, but eventually her body rebelled again and this time, when her body shut down it was much more drastic. She ended up in the hospital for over a week with one awful night spent in a psych ward. It turned out to be a blessing in disguise. The short term repercussions of that situation ended up with Haley being admitted for inpatient treatment and ultimately led to her and her husband getting a divorce. The long term benefit far outweighs the short term problems because Haley has now been in treatment for several years and is truly on her way to a life worth living.

Having experienced 3 separate instances of eating disorder symptoms and treatment, I learned a lot! Initially, I thought it was just a 'teenage thing' and she would grow out of it. The second time around, I continued thinking that it was a 'young adult thing' and that it was all about fitting in with the other college girls. It took until the third time around for me to realize that this had nothing to do with food or how she looked or whether or not she fit in. Symptom use (bingeing, purging, refusing to eat or drink) is what we see, but the problem lies much deeper. That's why treatment is crucial. I can't pretend (nor do I want) to understand every aspect of the disease, but there are experts who do understand and have dedicated their lives to helping people with eating disorders.

My advice to anyone who is supporting a friend or family member with an eating disorder is really very simple. Connect with the one you love. That can be through many different avenues such as spending time with them, talking to them, sending encouraging notes or cards. Support is so critical because they may feel very much alone in their journey. Whatever you can do to help them see the unconditional nature of your love and support will help.

On a practical note, one of the most important things that I learned was that if I had questions, all I needed to do was ask. Haley was very willing to answer my questions, even when

I thought they were stupid. That may not be the case for all eating disorder patients, so if you can't ask the patient, connect with someone on his/her support team. Another practical piece of advice is to remember to take care of yourself. It's not easy being a support person when dealing with a long term illness. If you neglect to care for yourself, you can't care for your loved one. I have been very blessed to have Haley's sister available as part of Haley's support team – we are not only able to vent to one another, but we've also developed a 'tag-team' approach to supporting Haley. There are times when I simply don't have it in me to handle the gamut of emotions and issues that come with this disease. When that happens, I defer to her sister who has experienced the same things. When she gets overwhelmed, that's when she 'tags' me and I step in.

I don't have all the answers – if I did, I would use them to cure this illness for all who deal with it! What I do know is that without love and support from friends and family, the eating disorder will take over and the results could very well be tragic.

My Younger Sister:

I never thought I would be writing my side of this story. A part of me has always known that Haley would put her story on paper to help others who had similar struggles, however, I didn't think that my role was significant enough to be featured. One of the things that I've learned throughout this journey is that support persons can greatly impact the struggle and recovery of a loved one with an eating disorder. In fact, it is a prominent factor in their long term success.

Because of our age difference (me being the younger sister by 6 years), I don't remember much of the early stages of Haley's eating disorder. I remember that she was always fairly withdrawn, but I thought that was just the "moody teenager" phase. My memory of her college years, however, is very clear. I remember her coming home from college with her new fiancé, and thinking that she looked so different. Her skin looked like it was barely holding her bones together, like her frail form could snap at the slightest nudge. Her hipbones were holding her pants in place and her cheeks were sunken deep into her face. She looked skeletal. It was difficult to see her like that, but what was harder to accept, was that she was proud of that "accomplishment." She told me how she and her fiancé were spending hours in the gym and that she'd worked very hard to be able to show off this new figure of hers. I was stunned and concerned.

She went on to marry her fiancé and after some time passed, I realized that I would only get the chance to see my sister on rare occasions – maybe 3-5 times a year. The reason for this was that her husband counted my family and I as an unhealthy influence on her. I missed her terribly, but it seemed like nothing could change the situation, so I resigned to that fact. Years later, something did change. I still remember the exact place that I was standing when I got the phone call that turned my world sideways. All of the sudden, the room was spinning and I was doubting my ability to process information. A medical emergency placed Haley in the hospital, and looked like it would greatly alter her way of life.

The next few weeks were very scary and contained a lot of tests and medical jargon that I didn't quite grasp, but the bottom line was, my sister had been slowly killing her body with her eating disorder.

She went into a recovery program dedicated to treating eating disorders, which gave me a great deal of hope. This is where my supporter role started to grow exponentially. I would go visit her while she was in treatment. We spent time doing the things we've always loved to do together. We colored, played board games, watched movies, and ate our meals together. I asked her an innumerable amount of questions about what she was learning in treatment, because I desperately wanted to be able to do everything right in helping her recover.

I soon found out that being the perfect supporter wasn't realistic. I made mistakes. I said things that triggered her eating disorder. Sometimes I didn't know what to say at all. But as she's told me again and again, being there for her was the best, and only thing I could do to help. I couldn't take the eating disorder away from her. I will never be able to do that. But I could let her know that she isn't fighting this battle alone.

Some time into her treatment, her husband decided that he wasn't cut out for a life with someone in recovery. After their divorce, she moved home and my supporter role increased again. I helped her with her meal plan while she was home (she still ate most of her meals at treatment). I made sure she knew that she was surrounded with love. Every night before she went to bed, I rubbed her back and read her favorite Psalm (Psalm 91).

While it was definitely challenging, I was thrilled to have my sister back. Throughout this journey, we've become best friends.

Being a supporter of a person with an eating disorder is not a simple task. The "job description" changes regularly. In one moment, I might be a comforter, and in the next, I could be a cheerleader. After that, I might need to be a listener. In all of those moments though, the most important role I played was hand-holder. I can't take this journey for her, but I will do everything in my power to help her along the way because I know that while being a supporter is hard at times, this battle is exceedingly harder for her every day.

PART TWO

What I wish I had known from the beginning: Myths, Facts, and Stories.

QUIZ: T/F

__ If you know what diagnosis your loved one has, you will know the ins and outs of their eating disorder.

__ There are well-defined steps that you can take to prevent an eating disorder from affecting your loved one.

__ Eating disorders are about food and body image.

__ People with eating disorders are vain and selfish.

__ Bulimia and Anorexia are the only *real* eating disorders.

__ It is possible for you (as the support person) to fix this problem for your loved one.

__ Men don't get eating disorders.

__ Once the behaviors are under control, the eating disorder is cured.

__ If your loved one loses a battle with their eating disorder, they have lost the war.

__ One day your loved one will be recovered and will be able to walk away from the eating disorder.

__ If your loved one is committed enough and works hard enough recovery will come easily.

__ You can tell what eating disorder someone has by the way that they look, and their size indicates how sick they are.

Answers: F, F, F, F, F... yeah they are all false.

4 DIAGNOSIS

MYTH:

If you know what diagnosis your loved one has, you will know the ins and outs of their eating disorder.

TRUTH:

It is important to know and remember that all eating disorders are unique to the individual. The patient themselves are the only person who can tell you what is really going on. Books and pamphlets are helpful and are an important tool, but there is really no better resource than your loved one from which to learn.

Communication is often very hard for both parties when the stakes are this high. You may feel lost and you may not know what to say or do, but having an open dialogue about the struggles of the person will provide more insight for you to work with. Coming to your loved one out of curiosity and love will often help them feel secure enough to talk to you. Aggressively addressing your loved one can be counterproductive, causing them to be defensive or to shut down. In the same vein, assuming that you know about their specific disorder because you read a web article about it can be invalidating. Try to keep in mind that your loved one is unique and while you have done your research, they (and their doctor) are the final two cents in the matter.

Eating disorders are cloaked in shame and doused in pain; people who suffer with this disease are often prone to isolation and extreme self-hatred; taking this into account will aid you in effectively communicating.

When you talk to your loved one, they may not respond the way you had hoped. Try not to get discouraged, be assured that you have done your part by planting a seed of support in their mind and heart. Some day they may come to you on their own terms with the knowledge that you are approachable and that you left that door open.

Survivor Story: Mindy – 22 years old

I have had bulimia since I was about 13 years old, though my symptoms differ from the traditional description of bulimia nervosa. I began restricting at first and then began exercising excessively to eliminate calories. After I got into a routine, I found that I wasn't losing weight as fast as I had wanted and it became a never ending obsession. At that point, I began purging. I have never binged in my life, though if I told you "I have bulimia", it would seem that I do because it is one of the diagnostic trademarks of bulimia. The general diagnosis does not give information on the struggles that I have, or who I am as a person.

When I was first diagnosed, my mom told me that she thought I only had part of an eating disorder since I only act on 'half' of the diagnosis. I understand that this came from a place of denial and fear on her part, but I felt like she didn't care.

It is frustrating to be put into a diagnostic box sometimes, as it feels that I am just a description of my coping mechanism. I have to remember that a diagnosis is merely a way for my doctor to talk to my insurance and to other care providers.

As I have grown I have accepted that I am more than a 'bulimic'. Now that I am an adult, I have chosen to receive professional treatment for my eating disorder. It is not easy but it is definitely worth it.

HELPFUL TIP: Asking open ended questions such as: "What did you do that was fun today?" will keep conversation flowing; where closed ended questions (those that elicit one word answers) tend to thwart conversation. When you show genuine interest in a person, they are more apt to be open and honest with you. Take a breath, remember that they are your loved one, not an alien, and be real.

5 PREVENTION

MYTH:

There are well-defined steps that you can take to prevent an eating disorder from affecting your loved one.

TRUTH:

Due to the fact that every human is different, there are no definitive steps to preventing your loved one from developing an eating disorder. Research has suggested that people can have a genetic predisposition to developing an eating disorder. It is the age old "nature vs. nurture" conundrum, and there is no solid, concrete answer as to which is more prevalent.

Also, the myth that there is something you could have done to prevent it, suggests that the problem is your fault, which is absolutely not true. Eating disorders are not anyone's fault, they happen, much like cancer, asthma, or allergies. They are terrible and life threatening, and blaming anyone for it is a waste of the energy that could have been used in the fight against the eating disorder.

Now that we have the monkey off of your back, it is important to know that there are things you CAN do to help set your loved one up for success. Think of it as deciding to take precautions so that you don't crash your car. Cars still crash, that's why they are called 'accidents' and not 'on purposes', but you can do whatever is in your power to prevent them on your end.

I am absolutely not an authority on parenting or raising children, all I am is a grown up child that had a strong learning curve with her parents. Here are some things that you can do that may prove helpful no matter the age of your loved one:

- Focus on who the person is, not what they do. (i.e.: If they play a sport, congratulate them on the win and understand their disappointment on a loss, encourage them to grow, AND note how proud you are that they are dedicated, loyal, and have good work ethic.) Nagging and harping will not encourage healthy growth and solid behavior in your loved one; it will only instill fear and insecurity. Negative attention may motivate them to change in the short term, but it doesn't facilitate positive long term growth.

- Encourage balanced eating and healthy activity without being critical of their physical shape or energy level (especially if they are young). Consistency is the key. Teaching this once will not be effective. Modeling and consistent application of the principles will foster long term learning. Understanding how to trust one's body's signals like tired, hungry, full, etc., in everyday life is paramount in building a healthy rapport with food and exercise. It also enhances a person's confidence in their whole being, creates a shameless view of their worth, and equips them to be resilient in a world that is critical, image focused, and sometimes cruel.

- Monkey see, Monkey do: If you are always yo-yo dieting and critical of your body and others around you, your loved one will probably follow suit.

Last but not least, LISTEN to your loved one. The way that they talk will often give you clues to how they are coping with life, and how they see themselves. Are they engaging in self-deprecating talk or being overly critical of themselves? How do they relate with the people around them? Many times our judgments of others come from our own insecurities about ourselves. Open ended questions will be helpful here. Asking questions like: "I'm curious what you mean by that?" or "Can you tell me more about that? I'm interested in hearing why you think that." show that you are interested and invested in who they are as a person.

If you do find that they have an eating disorder, try not to beat yourself up. Remember that it isn't your fault, or theirs.

Survivor Story: Julia – 17 years old

My parents knew that something was wrong with my eating and relationship to food when I was about 14, but they were too busy to say anything. They were also confused, so instead of talking to me, they became more consumed in work. I felt like the air was thick every time we ate together (which wasn't often). The conversations that we did have were strained and superficial, often revolving around the weather and sports.

I craved attention from them, but didn't know how to ask for it. Communication was not our strong suit. Through trial and error, I realized that I got attention when I did well in basketball and softball. I made it a point to succeed at both, which kept me busy all year long. The more I won, the more they would pay attention – it was a pretty simple equation. I became consumed in sports; I worked out more, ate less, took supplements and eventually ended up in the hospital. Not only was I losing focus, I was also miserable. I started to wonder if this was worth the effort. I decided that this was not the attention that I was looking for.

While I was in the hospital, my parents and I learned that I was in the throes of an eating disorder. They weren't very surprised about the diagnosis, but they were confused about how I 'got' it. It was not my parents' fault that I developed an eating disorder, rather a lack of understanding and communication which manifested as such. I wish we had all known the warning signs. My diagnosis and subsequent treatment changed a lot of things in my life. Now my parents and I talk about things, we make time to see each other, and we are all committed to fighting the eating disorder. We don't always get along, but we are all on the same team now.

HELPFUL HINT: None of this is done in one conversation. Patience, consistency, and validation will get you much further than quickly or impatiently trying to 'fix' the person or problem.

6 AND THAT'S WHAT IT'S ALL ABOUT…

MYTH

Eating disorders are about food and body image.

TRUTH

More often than not, an eating disorder is a symptom of a deeper issue. It is a coping mechanism used to deal with painful and intense feelings, and to make sense of the world. It's a desperate plea for the ingredients of a life worth living, such as: love, attention, safety, understanding, stability, credibility, intimacy, and more.

I can't count the times that I have heard someone say "Oh My Gosh, she is so skinny – would someone get that girl a cheeseburger??" Normally it is said as a joke, but it implies two things: All skinny people starve themselves, and if someone isn't eating, food will fix the problem. Neither of these assumptions are true, rather, they are very inaccurate and can be quite damaging.

For me, the eating disorder served very specific purposes: It provided security - I knew what to expect, and had something to work at. I felt like food and my body were the only two things that I had control over. It helped me excel at keeping people at arm's length due to the fact that I was terrified of criticism and abandonment, and it kept me numb to flashbacks and nightmares stemming from earlier trauma. My eating disorder helped me appear "put together" and "in control of my life", which served me in my career, and also pushed everyone away from me. No one can relate with perfection or the illusion thereof. Lastly, but definitely not least... it was a way for me to cope with the shame that I felt from just being 'me' – If only I were different, I would be loved, safe, successful, etc. The eating disorder fueled my perfectionism, made me lonelier, and almost killed me.

On the surface, I was concerned with calories, weight, workouts, numbers, and my shape, but what was really broken was my heart. My inner pain is what was driving the obsession with the physical. So, yes, on the outside eating disorders can seem food and body related, but really they are a symptom of something deeper.

Survivor Story: Jennifer – 29 year old

When I told my friends that I had an eating disorder, they weren't surprised, though they were admittedly uneducated in the area. They, like many others, wanted to jump in and support me in any way possible. It seemed that invitations for dinner, coffee dates, and lunches were coming out of the woodwork. My friends thought that keeping me accountable and watching me eat, would make the disorder go away, much like a phase or a passing fad. They assumed that I would eventually 'get over it'.

I did end up seeking out treatment and I worked very hard at following the meal plan and managing my other symptoms. I started to restore weight and the people around me made comments like "I am so happy to see that the eating disorder is going away!" and "You look so healthy, thank God you are over it." It was important that I explained to them that my appearance and caloric intake were not a barometer for the severity of my eating disorder. It is still a struggle when people don't understand, and sometimes I feel invalidated and misunderstood but I know that this is a learning curve for everyone involved. I try to give them grace and understand that they aren't living in my shoes. I assure them that I am doing what I can to recover, and that I am an open book if they want to know more.

HELPFUL HINT: It is easy for support to think that the meal plan is the cure-all. "If only my loved one would eat in a balanced fashion, then they will no longer suffer from an eating disorder." This thought is logical but also the furthest from the truth. Telling someone to eat a balanced diet will not fix the problem. Food will help them be strong enough to cope with the core issues, and following a monitored meal plan is an excellent (and necessary) first step, but food is not the problem or the answer. Also, their body image will not be resolved by just accepting that they are beautiful. Body image is helped when self-image is worked on.

7 VANITY

MYTH

People with eating disorders are vain and selfish.

TRUTH

The assumption that eating disorder patients are vain and/or selfish is very common, and couldn't be more wrong. Many people with eating disorders are intense people pleasers; they often unknowingly put themselves at risk to cater to others. It is common for someone with an eating disorder to be extremely insecure with how they look and who they are as a person regardless of complements suggesting otherwise.

It is very contradictory; on the surface, patients can seem wholly image focused and self-important, however, they are actually frantically trying to convince themselves and others that they aren't worthless and ugly. We have all had the friend who is beautiful and intelligent, but constantly asks for validation regarding their worth. People with a negative self-image have a hard time believing in their positive qualities regardless of what their friends and family keep telling them. A lot of times, these people will look for validation from friends or sexual partners. On one hand, anything that confirms their core beliefs can be devastating and on the other, people with negative self-image may habitually choose partners who validate their core belief, often ending up abused and hurt.

If anything is vain and selfish, it is the eating disorder itself. It will take advantage of your loved one for its benefit, it will ruin every system in their body, it will force its ideology on him or her, and it will steal their life if not adequately addressed.

Survivor Story: Clara – 25 years old

When I am engrossed in my eating disorder, I am overly obsessed with my appearance and consumed by my own thoughts. I know that I come off as a selfish ice queen, and

I am really ashamed of it. When I am not isolating, I am asking people if I am fat or if I look good just to get some sort of relief from the incessant voice in my head saying that I am worthless. I am actually terrified that one day, someone is going to agree with my self-evaluation. I would rather that people see the ice queen just so they won't get close enough to realize that I am an empty shell. I wish I could convey that I am hurting and terrified, but I can't, so I try to make sure that I fix my flaws – thighs, stomach, hair, arms, makeup, clothes. I really do care about others and I wish that was apparent. I hate that this disorder uses these insecurities against me, and that the insecurities perpetuate the eating disorder. I am appalled by what this monster makes me look like... literally and figuratively speaking.

Helpful Hint: Asking someone how they feel will be more encouraging than telling them how they look. When one's body changes in treatment, it is often mortifying. Focusing on the person apart from the image and disorder is really helpful.

8 'REAL' EATING DISORDERS

MYTH

Bulimia and Anorexia are the only *real* eating disorders.

TRUTH

The fact is that there are a handful of diagnosis and millions of variations of those.

A diagnosis is simply a term to explain what is going on in one's life/body/behavior. It is a way that doctors and insurance companies can communicate, and a way for health providers to have a rough idea of what the patient is dealing with. Unfortunately there is an unspoken hierarchy that exists not only in the eating disorder community but in society as well. People assume that anorexia is more severe than bulimia and that bulimia is more severe than EDNOS, furthermore, there is a belief that BED is not dangerous at all. Let me be clear: There is no 'better' or 'worse' eating disorder to have, they are all deadly.

As far as support persons are concerned, diagnosis can really be a pain in the tookus, and difficult to grapple with. Having the attitude that your loved one doesn't have a 'real' eating disorder because they are not 'anorexic' or 'bulimic' can be very damaging. It not only sets a black and white view of the problem in your own head, it can also invalidate your loved one by either showing them that you don't take their struggle seriously, or give them a false sense of health and safety: "If I don't have anorexia or bulimia, I'm fine." This attitude can poison a relationship between supporters and supported, and can fuel an already destructive disorder. Although it is not logical, one of the struggles that patients face is the competition of who is sickest... If you don't look or sound sick enough, you may not be able to get help, and if you are very 'sick' then somehow you are more deserving of the attention and resources necessary to live. This isn't a cut and dried illness. With cancer, you have cancer cells making it undeniable that the patient is sick. With an eating disorder, the problem is physical and mental with the physical evidence often lacking. A great way to deal with this issue is to realize how important your loved one is apart from their diagnosis, notice that they are a person struggling with a disease that is trying to kill them.

Survivor Story: Monica – 36 years old

I have been diagnosed once with Anorexia, and once with EDNOS (eating disorder not otherwise specified). The change came when I no longer fulfilled the whole diagnostic criteria for anorexia… in other words, I wasn't 'underweight' enough, so according to the diagnostic gods, I did not fit into a specific category, so I got put into the 'there is no specific definition, or category for your symptoms, but you still have an eating disorder' diagnosis (EDNOS). It is really hard not to feel invalidated when I think about being in limbo. I'm not anorexic and I'm not bulimic, but I'm still afflicted. Sometimes I feel like I have failed at recovery and at having an eating disorder because my body doesn't reflect the abuse that I put it through. The stereotypes that run rampant about eating disorders are really hurtful sometimes because I feel like I'm not taken seriously when I am in so much emotional turmoil. Part of me feels like having EDNOS means that I am fat (not logical I know). When I use my wise mind, I recognize that an eating disorder is an eating disorder is an eating disorder. Also, I know that I am not my diagnosis; I am a strong, beautiful and unique woman – even if I don't believe it all of the time.

Helpful Hint: It is important that you recognize the struggle, regardless of how that is demonstrated in their life. The diagnosis doesn't matter, the person does.

9 MR. FIX-IT

MYTH

It is possible for you (as the support person) to fix this problem for your loved one.

TRUTH

You can absolutely help the person in your life that is struggling, but no one, other than themselves can take the steps necessary to walk into recovery. Unfortunately, when people are hurting, it is very easy for them to point the finger at the people closest to them, and you could be the target. At some point you will probably feel that you are being blamed for your loved one's issues, which may lead you to accept responsibility and try to 'fix it' out of supporter guilt. You could also be so offended that you back up and reconsider whether you can be a support person at all. Give yourself and your loved one some grace. Remember that it is not your fault, and that you are doing your best.

We (the supported) say mean things to our supporters sometimes and it is important to realize that the attacks are not from us per se, rather from the eating disorder. Accusations and attacks are coming out of a place of hurt, fear, and desperation. This is one of the hardest parts of being a support person, and you are not alone. Sometimes it will feel like you can't seem to do anything right, but that is not the truth, because there is no right or wrong way to support someone… Let me repeat that: THERE IS NO RIGHT OR WRONG WAY TO SUPPORT SOMEONE. You do the best you can, and take it one day at a time. You will soon realize that the light at the end of the tunnel is, in fact, sunlight, and not a train barreling towards you.

While eating disorders can be bullies, supporters do not have to, and should not put up with abuse. If you feel like you are being mistreated, describe the problem, express how you are feeling, and set boundaries pertaining to what is acceptable behavior. Make it clear as to what you will and won't tolerate. It also may be helpful for you to seek out a support group or therapist so you can stay mentally healthy during this time.

EATING DISORDER CONFESSION: I am the first to admit that I have been stubborn, mean, cruel, belligerent, obnoxious, and horrible to my support at times. I continue to apologize to them to this day because I know that their job is HARD and sometimes my eating disorder gets the best of me and lashes out. Supporters: Try to remember that your loved one isn't trying to hurt you, take a deep breath, stand your ground, and give them a hug. By doing this, you are not only taking care of yourself, you are also showing them that you understand them on some level.

Supporter Story: Susan – 50 years old

When my daughter told me that she was struggling with an eating disorder at 22 years old, I panicked. As a parent, I felt like I had failed at protecting my daughter and I went into 'fix-it' mode. I thought that making her meals, checking on her constantly, monitoring treatment outcomes, and managing her workouts would could fix it – if not *for* her – I could do it with her. I threw myself into researching and controlling and found that my efforts were counterproductive. The more that I pushed, the more she pushed back. The more I controlled, the more she isolated. When I got angry, she shut me out. My daughter didn't need me to fix her, she needed me to love and accept her. When we both realized what she needed, things became more cohesive and we began mending our relationship.

For me, supporting no longer means taking frantic stabs in the dark, it means asking how she is doing, hugging her when she is down, and asking (and accepting) what she needs from me.

Helpful Hint: It is important that you know yourself and your own boundaries. It is okay to say that you are not in a place that is conducive to supporting someone. It is better to know that about yourself and help your loved one find help, than to push yourself and end up sick as well.

10 A LADIES DISEASE

MYTH

Men don't get eating disorders.

TRUTH

According to the National Eating Disorders Association, ten million males in America will suffer from an eating disorder at some point in their lives. This is not a women's illness. There are many factors that affect body image and the motivation to control weight in men, such as societal pressure to be muscular and fit, sports that encourage men to maintain unrealistic weights in order to perform, and sexuality. Sports such as football, wrestling, body building, and skiing can have strict body size and weight requirements. So much so that men are driven to artificially manipulate their bodies. The idea that eating disorders are a gay man's problem is also false. Gay men make up 42% of all men with eating disorders in America. Eating disorders are an equal opportunity disease, affecting every type of human.

One of my best friends is a straight male with a huge future ahead of him, has a heart of gold, AND he has battled an eating disorder. His eating disorder almost killed him. I met him shortly after he began the walk into recovery. It was a long battle, and affected every area of his life. He now lives a life out from under the oppression of his eating disorder. He still struggles daily with urges to use the coping mechanism, but he chooses not to. He is enjoying a life worth living, and I couldn't be happier for him. This is his story:

Survivor Story: Dave – 30 years old

It is true that no two eating disorders are alike, even if the medical diagnoses are the same. One of the defining factors is the origin of each person's struggle. I was raised by a single parent without any contact from my father. Mental illness runs in my family and I also dealt with childhood obesity, self-confidence issues, and an abusive marriage that ended in a divorce. The combination of these events and personal predispositions initiated my drive to become 'healthy'. First, I decided to quit smoking, and then when I achieved that, I decided to lose weight. At some point, 'healthy' became an obsession and was a game of numbers. The more weight I lost, the better I felt about myself and my life. I became addicted to weight loss via the chemical reactions of pleasure in my brain – not much different than the high from alcohol or drugs. My eating disorder was then born and started taking over my entire life.

As my weight continued to drop, my body's natural instinct for survival took over. My body weight was too low, which affected my ability to control what, and how much, I put in my mouth. At first, I feared that I would revert to my old overweight self. This fear motivated me to have 'self-control' which would last a few days to a week until my body took over once again. After a few years, I could no longer control myself during the day. I would eat massive amounts of food, until I could not physically walk. To combat the effects of these binges, I would exercise for hours a day, take large quantities of diet pills, and I abused laxatives. The mixture of these symptoms should have killed me. I sought professional help at an inpatient treatment center.

While professionals know what they are doing, recovery also takes a great deal of personal effort, honesty and trust. The other thing that helps recovery progress is a great deal of support. I'm not talking about a call once in a while (thought that is still important), I am talking the kind of support that is there twenty-four hours a day, that will not react negatively, or judge you for what you are saying or going through. This nonjudgmental stance is important because no one truly knows exactly what someone may be feeling, even if the supporter has an eating disorder as well. Again this speaks to the unique nature of this disease. My family and friends supported me and reassured me throughout my fight, and reminded me that no matter what I looked like or what I was going though, they would be there and the struggle wouldn't change how much they loved and cared for me.

Through it all, I have reached a place of recovery, and still strive to get to a place where I can say I am recovered. I don't know if I will ever get there, or if it even exists, despite that thought, I continue to try. Recovery has come in stages. At first, I asked for help, then there was ceasing to use symptoms, then came rigid structure, and finally listening to my body and living 'normally'. These stages aren't the same for everyone, and they are not static. I have bounced between them, and will continue to do so as I continue on my recovery journey. The fact that eating disorders and recovery are unique to the individual makes it difficult for treatment teams to assess the issue and develop effective treatment plans.

Helpful Hint: No matter whom you are or what you struggle with, there is relief and even an answer. It takes hard work, but it is worth it. To the supporters, keep hanging on, and know that your job is so important and that you aren't alone.

11 NO SYMPTOM, NO PROBLEM

MYTH

Once the behaviors are under control, the eating disorder is cured.

TRUTH

Remember Shrek? Remember how ogres are like onions? Well, people are like onions, and those with eating disorders have many layers that need to be addressed in order to recover from this disease. When the eating disorder symptoms (whatever they may be) are in check, the patient is then able to work on the next layer of issues which run the gamut from abandonment issues, abuse, gender confusion, co-occurring disorders, trauma, family dynamics and more.

Getting symptoms under control is a huge accomplishment which deserves much praise. It is also where the work begins. No one can work on deeper problems if they are malnourished, under-rested, chemically imbalanced, and unable to carry out daily functions. This is one of the ways that eating disorders have a perceived 'pay off', they allow the sufferer to stay as far away from the center of the onion as possible. The deeper things are scary, and often times it seems that they are too hard to deal with. This is also one reason that relapse is so prevalent. A patient may get to a place where they are ready to dig deeper and then get overwhelmed a while into it and revert to eating disordered behaviors. Sometimes it is a quick slip, and sometimes it takes a while to get back on track. Either way, once the patient is ready, therapy on the deeper issues will commence.

Survivor Story: Chantel – 19 years old

My dad was an alcoholic for as long as I could remember. Generally he was a happy drunk, but when he was mean, he was *really* mean. There were many times that I watched him beat my mother into submission and the fear of that drove me to shut down. I learned to cope by bingeing after everyone had gone to bed. I felt so out of control, but it gave me an outlet for the fear, and helped me feel full and safe.

After I went to college, I started gaining weight, and it wasn't slowing down. I realized that I was sick and shortly thereafter, I sought treatment for binge eating disorder. I was so ashamed, and therapy was very hard because I didn't trust anyone. When I felt ready, I told my family about the symptoms and about my treatment. They were not very receptive – probably because it shone a light on their issues and shortcomings.

When I had the bingeing under control, my therapist started to work with me on the things that caused me to cope in that way. Oh my gosh, I though getting over the symptoms was hard, the internal work that came next was brutal. It hurt to remember the abuse and the pain and to come to terms with the illness that my dad suffers from.

I had to learn how to deal with the feelings of anger, abandonment, fear, rage, etc. I also needed to grieve the relationship with him and the dreams of having a loving and nurturing father.

My parents are no longer together. His illness tore our family apart and I'm now trying to repair things with both of my parents separately.

On the outside, I look recovered, but the reality is that I have a long way to go in order to recover from this disorder. I recognize that the hard work is balanced by a growing sense of freedom and joy and this realization helps when I feel hopeless. If I don't focus on the positive outcome, I lose motivation to keep working. I have faith that this journey will be worth it.

Note: It is really common for families to have multi-generational disease, and that includes mental illness. It is not uncommon for a person to be diagnosed with and eating disorder, and others in the family to come out about depression, anxiety, or other mental illness as well. It is not a bad thing, or something to judge a family by, it just 'is what it is.' Getting help for anyone struggling is of utmost importance.

12 BATTLEFIELD

MYTH

If your loved one loses a battle with their eating disorder, they have lost the war.

TRUTH

Recovering from an eating disorder is accomplished by fighting many battles. These battles happen weekly, daily, and sometimes hourly. Like any war, some battles are lost and some battles are won.

George A. Custer said: "It's not how many times you get knocked down that matters, it's how many times you get back up."

Success comes from getting knocked down 8 times and getting back up 9 times. The road to recovery is not a straight line, it is full of twists, turns and detours, often including relapses, periods of recovery, and sometimes living in a limbo stage where the eating disorder seems dormant, but not gone.

You can bless your loved one by helping them cultivate grace within themselves, reminding them of the progress they have made, and encouraging them to make the next right move, even if that means 8 ounces of water and a granola bar.

The best gift my mom ever gave me was something that she said while I was sobbing on her couch. I was crying because I needed to eat half of a muffin and drink a glass of milk to fulfill my meal plan. I was terrified of the food and mortified that I was reacting in this way. She looked at me and said "I am so proud of you, you are working so hard, and there is a breakthrough on the horizon. You can do this." That is all she had to say for me to understand that I was not, in fact, alone in what seemed like an impossible fight. I continued to struggle with that snack, but knowing that she wasn't judging me helped ease the embarrassment.

Survivor Story: Charlotte – 39 years old

I have lived the squiggly line of recovery. I have gone from limbo, to recovery, then relapsed and thought that I failed. Each time that things got wobbly, I got back up and after years of doing so, I realized that every breakdown leads to a breakthrough.

One of the beauties of the human spirit is that there is always a small voice that whispers “Get back up, do it again”. So, I work towards recovery again, listening to the professionals, working my program, gaining confidence, and making real strides. Then a few years later, when everything seems to be going smoothly, something happens and BAM... relapse. I have come to find that the goal is not perfection, it is progress. I accept now, that as long as there is an upward trend, there is progress being made. Every time I slip ‘backward’, I learn something new, I uncover something else, and I become stronger. The only defeat found in the fight for recovery is death.

Helpful Hint: Every war takes equipment – shields, weapons, footwear, helmets, armor, courage, strength, and many people. Recovery is much like this, do what you can to fill your toolbox with all of the gear that you think would help fight this war.

13 TALK TO THE HAND

MYTH

One day your loved one will be recovered and will be able to walk away from the eating disorder.

TRUTH

Recovery is absolutely possible, and people with eating disorders can move on... however, it is believed that this battle is much like alcoholism in that the urges to fall back into a pattern of disordered behavior will always be there to some degree.

I heard once that recovering from an eating disorder is like driving a car. At first, ED (the acronym for eating disorder) is in the driver's seat, being reckless and endangering your life. When you acknowledge him and take steps to oust him, you decide to take your life back into your own hands, and ED moves to the passenger seat. Now that he is next to you, he is doing everything that he can to distract you from the road and make you follow his directions (often shows up as anxiety, anger, frustration, and increased symptoms). After focusing on the road (working a committed program for a while), you are less distracted and able to roll your eyes, selectively blocking ED out. You have had enough of it and move him to the backseat – still annoying, but easier to ignore. At this point, you have started to add positive things into your life, which fill up all of the seats in your car (hobbies, loved ones, things you lost to the eating disorder), and ED ends up in the trunk. You can hear him kicking every now and then, but you are focused on the road and the joyful people in your car which makes his influence a muffled noise, similar to that of rocks under your tires, or dogs barking on the next block.

This is often times how recovery goes, ED will move to different parts of the car, but the longer a person persists on the road to recovery, practices other coping skills, and learns to ignore him, the quieter he will be. As your loved one builds skills for living and becomes less vulnerable to ED's attacks, this battle will get easier and easier.

In my experience, I have found that recovery comes in fits and starts. It is something I work at actively and with purpose. I am a driven person and I put a lot of pressure on myself to do things perfectly – recovery was no different. When I relapsed, I was so ashamed and almost gave up because I believed that I had failed. As I have grown, I've found that my recovery is a daily choice - a choice to say no to symptoms, and say yes to a life worth living. There may be a day where I am 'recovered', but until then, I will live recovery in my heart and actions on a daily basis. As far as 'moving on', I choose to look at it as moving forward, making sure that my experiences lift me to a new level even if they trip me up temporarily.

Michaela has lived the ups and downs of recovery in a way that many people do – with co-occurring disorders and a propensity for 'addiction hopping'. Here is her story.

Survivor Story: Michaela – 35 years old

I started having maladaptive coping skills back in high school. All the years leading up to that, I had never felt "enough". You name it... I didn't feel smart enough, pretty enough, thin enough, and athletic enough, loved enough, or appreciated enough.

When I couldn't deal with that feeling, I started harming myself as a way of releasing some pent up stress. When I realized that I was leaving permanent scars and felt the extreme shame that those scars caused, I experimented with alcohol and marijuana. With these substances, I felt like I had arrived at what life was supposed to be. Off to the races! My life felt complete, like I belonged. I was funny, smart, pretty, thin, strong... almost superhuman! I loved this feeling for a long time until I got pregnant at age 18.

Growing up sucked. I had to get a real job, support a family and resign to the fact that the fun in my life was gone. I found myself in a familiar place again – not good enough, not thin enough, and just not enough. I felt like a little girl in a big girl's world – faking it until I was going to make it.

I started working in a plastic surgery practice and felt like a kid in a candy store. After three liposuctions, breast implants, and having my nose done, I still felt lacking. I ended up three kids deep, tackling a full time career, and surviving an unhappy marriage. I began to drink again. The alcohol helped me feel more normal, but I knew that if I was just thinner, I would be complete and happy.

After a very long weekend in Vegas with girlfriends, I realized I was an alcoholic and would die if I didn't stop drinking. That was officially 'enough'! "Now what? Gah!! How do I deal with this feeling of not enough again?" My skin crawled. I hated everything and I quickly learned a new coping mechanism – bulimia. I jumped in head first, I was all in, no wading, just doing it. I was sober, but still dying.

Bulimia consumed every waking minute of my life for 12 years. Forty pound weight fluctuations resulted in comments from friends and family to the effect of "Is she terminally ill?" and "Are you a professional body builder?" I was so offended, I just wanted to say "Um, no – I have a severe eating disorder and am in and out of every treatment modality out there... but thanks."

I was still sober though... Yay me! (Eye roll)

I began to learn to live on life's terms and to believe in a power greater than myself through 12 step groups like AA and EDA (alcoholics anonymous and eating disorders anonymous). I learned to 'do the next right thing' which meant that even when I messed up, I had a choice to start over in that moment. I started to be grateful and started seeing the gifts given to me. I lost friends to addiction and realized that I was killing myself in a slow and painful way.

I have had many spiritual awakenings, or as some call them 'God moments'. I invite God to be with me many times every day and if I am quiet in my heart, ignoring the committee in my head, I feel Him with me.

Today, I am 13 years sober. I am still working in plastic surgery and have been for over 20 years. I love my job for the gifts it gives others, it is so much more than cosmetic, and these procedures can change lives. I have been divorced and I am now married to my best friend and have 3 great kids who are self-sufficient and looking forward to life. I am healthier, stronger, and more active than ever at age 40. I still struggle with thoughts of bingeing and purging, but it's too much effort now and I would rather do the next right thing.

Note: Keep your hopes up for recovery, that is a great way to stay motivated and to keep your loved one motivated, just keep your mind open to other problems that may be occurring as well.

14 COMMITTMENT

MYTH

If your loved one is committed enough and works hard enough, recovery will come easily.

TRUTH

Feelings of motivation come and go, and it is definitely a struggle when battling an eating disorder. In the fight against this disease, commitment comes in every single recovery-focused action. Every time your loved one moves toward recovery, it is an act of commitment. This is not true conversely. When they take a step sideways or 'backwards', it does not mean that they are *not* committed, it means that they hit a road bump and need support to move past it.

Also, sometimes it is not about working 'hard'. A lot of times, a life of recovery develops by learning to slow down, be mindful, and practice radical self-care. Essentially, an eating disorder is the lack of care for the body/mind that we have been given. Learning how to have compassion and love for one's body and mind is a very difficult task, and may sometimes seem impossible for the person struggling.

Encouraging your loved one to stop and breathe, to get a pedicure when stressed, to take a nap when they are tired, or to settle in with a good book when overwhelmed can serve them and you in a multitude of areas. This is HARD work, and it is constant. Being gentle with one's self while working toward recovery is vital to success.

This is one of the areas that may seem counterintuitive. You may wonder how taking a nap or getting a pedicure could be considered hard work. Our society tells us that long hours, physical sacrifice, and burnout are the markers of success. This is why self-care can seem so foreign and also why it is so important. Slow and steady work is still hard. No matter how committed someone is recovery is still a difficult process.

Survivor Story: Gwen – 29

For me, working hard enough and being committed enough is what got me so deep into the eating disorder. I am an over-achiever (like many of my eating disordered peers) and I was going to be the best at whatever I was tasked with – whether that was being thin, or climbing the corporate ladder, or recovering 'right'. My first attempt at recovery, I worked so hard and I was so driven to recover that I flew through treatment, and was almost in a manic mode about 'recovery'. (Imagine a little purple gremlin with googley eyes, running around in circles, pulling their hair out and screaming 'I'M RECOVERING BAHHHHHH!')... That was me.

What I didn't learn was how to care for my body at a practical and every day level. I knew all of the medical facts, and could recite the right things at the right times to the right people, but that didn't sustain my recovery. I was recovering intellectually, but the information failed to travel from my head to my heart. I was going through the motions, but when life threw me a curve ball, I crashed, and I crashed hard.

My recovery thus far was not life-proof, and I became burned out. I had to learn self-care. The things that work for me are spending time meditating, people watching, sitting around bonfires, and spending quality time with friends. I still struggle with caring for myself as I tend to feel guilty, but it is part of my journey and I can confidently say that I am making progress.

Helpful Hint: Have you noticed that some of this information is not intuitive? It is definitely a learning curve for you as the support, and also for your loved one. What should be common sense to you is often opposite, and in that vein, it is like learning a different lifestyle – trying to understand the world of an eating disorder. This is a disease, it doesn't make sense, but these nonsensical intricacies are key to your peace of mind and sanity. Coming to a realization that you can't, and they can't, do this process alone, or wrong, will serve you well. Again... grace.

15 GET THAT GIRL A CHEESEBURGER

MYTH

You can tell what eating disorder someone has by the way that they look, and their size indicates how sick they are.

TRUTH

I would argue that this is the biggest misconception about eating disorders. In plain words:

Weight has nothing to do with the health of someone struggling with an eating disorder.

Yes, one of the diagnostic criteria for anorexia is a stipulation about weight; however, all eating disorders are deadly. You could have anorexia, bulimia, binge eating disorder, EDNOS, or any other combination and have a similar chance of dying from it.

A few things that are unhelpful and commonly said are “They are not ‘that’ sick”, or “I’m not sick enough for treatment”, also, “She looks so anorexic”, or suggesting that thinner people “Just eat a cheeseburger”. All of these assumptions are 100% unfounded and false. I know thin people who don’t have an eating disorder, and I know average sized to larger people who are literally rotting from the inside-out. Eating disorders are serious diseases; in fact, they are the most deadly of all mental illnesses according to the national institutes of health.

Eating disorders affect every system in the body regardless of body fat percentage. They eat away at the heart and muscles, deprive the brain of necessary nutrients, dehydrate all of the cells, slow metabolic functioning, cause loss of concentration, deplete bone mass, cause an inability to make informed decisions, among many other things. Eating disorders can result in heart attacks, strokes, loss of teeth, osteoporosis, erosion of the gastrointestinal system, kidney failure, liver failure, severe depression and anxiety, and death.

All of the symptoms listed above are on the inside of the person… you cannot know how sick a person is by their body weight. I am 5'11" and I have a large bone structure. Most of my life, I have carried extra weight, AND I battle a very real eating disorder which has attempted to take my life at least 4 times in the past 25 years. At different times in my life, at all weights, including recent history, I have suffered from kidney damage, tachycardia, fainting spells which have resulted in driving difficulties, high and low blood pressure, marked confusion and memory loss, liver damage, muscle weakness, severe and chronic dehydration, and overwhelming self-hatred. All because of the eating disorder.

Helpful Hint: This takes some time to wrap one's head around. It's so hard as humans to not feel invincible. These things can happen to anyone, and just because the problems aren't showing up right now, doesn't mean that the long lasting damage won't be an issue 10, 20, or 30 years from now (which could be long after the eating disorder has gone dormant).

16 IN SUM…

You took the quiz at the beginning of our journey, and I hope that I have provided sufficient evidence to suggest that these myths are false. These are the main points that I stressed:

- Diagnoses are necessary for professionals to communicate with each other about patient's symptoms and struggles, but they do not in any way define your loved one.

- While there are things that you can do to set your loved one up for success, it's not possible for you to prevent an eating disorder. There are genetic and environmental components.

- Food issues and body image are the obvious markers of eating disorders; however they are not the main concern. This disease is used as a coping mechanism to deal with life's hurts.

- The only thing vain and selfish about an eating disorder is the disorder itself.

- There are many different kinds of eating disorders, all equally harmful and potentially deadly.

- You are a support person, not a healer. It is not your job to fix anything for your loved one. Pointing them in the direction of professional help, and assuring them that you are invested are the best things that you can do for them.

- Eating disorders are an equal opportunity disease. It does not discriminate based on sex, color, socio-economic status, sexuality, size, or any other dimension.

- Behaviors are the trademark of an eating disorder, but the real work begins when the behaviors are under control. The eating disorder is not gone once weight is restored, or when behaviors cease to be a problem.

- The fight against this disease is a war, not a single battle. Some battles will be won, some will be lost, and the only defeat is death.

- Recovery is a real thing! Continuing to balance hard work and self-care will result in a beautiful life with the eating disorder locked in the trunk. It may not be silent, but your loved one can go on without using it to cope.

- Self-care is vital to long term success. Eating disorders are notorious for sucking life dry of any enjoyment or pleasure. Reintroducing this into one's life will ensure that the hard work will pay off.

- Last but not least, please know that you cannot diagnose an eating disorder or determine its severity based on the physical characteristics of a patient.

The goal of every eating disorder – regardless of type – is to kill the affected. It is our job as both supporters and supported to team up against the eating disorder, because it is a life or death situation.

While these myths are not all encompassing, I have spent a lot of time interviewing people with and without eating disorders in order to come up with a 'top 10' of sorts. The myths that I chose to expand on are those that are often at the forefront of misunderstandings and cultural biases regarding the disease. These are the basics, there is a lot of research and many other authors, doctors, and professionals that you can learn from, and I encourage you to seek out more information if you are interested. I encourage you to do your own research, question your assumptions, and be open to new information

PART THREE

Resources

17 WHERE DO I GO FROM HERE?

If you or someone you know is struggling with an eating disorder, or you suspect that they may be, please seek help. It is not always appropriate to confront them right away. Do your research, ask a professional, and come to the problem with a potential solution. In the following pages, you will find websites and other resources that you can use to take the next steps.

I have not provided the names or information of any specific treatment program for two reasons. The first being that there are so many in the U.S. and abroad that it would be impossible to list them all in this little book. Secondly, I do not directly endorse any program over another. Choosing a treatment option is up to the patient and their support, and I feel I would be limiting your search for the 'right fit' if I were to give you a small list of programs.

Instead, I am giving you a list of resources where you can find information and literature. This can help you more fully understand eating disorders and the options that are out there for help. From there, you will be better informed on what qualities you are looking for in a treatment program.

This list is not all-encompassing, and we have amazing search engines on the internet, so please don't feel limited by this list, rather I encourage you to expand it if it works for you.

RESOURCES

N.E.D.A. National Eating Disorders Association
165 West 46th Street
Suite 402
New York, NY 10036
(212) 575-6200
Nationaleatingdisorders.org

C.O.P.E. Community Outreach for the Prevention of Eating Disorders
cope-ecf.org

Multi-Service Eating Disorders Association, Inc.
288 Walnut Street, Suite 130
Newton, MA 02460
617-558-1881
medainc.org

Academy for Eating Disorders
111 Deer Lake Road, Suite 100
Deerfield, IL 60015
847-498-4274
aedweb.org

Binge Eating Disorder Association
637 Emerson Place
Severna Park, MD 21146
855-855-2332
bedaonline.com

Body Image Health
2497 7th Avenue East, #109
North St. Paul, MN 55109
651-770-2693
bodyimageheath.org

Eating Disorder Hope
eatingdisorderhope.com

Eating Disorders Anonymous
eatingdisordersanonymous.org

Eating Disorder Referral and Information Center
edreferral@gmail.com
edreferral.com

F.E.A.S.T. Families Empowered & Supporting Treatment of Eating Disorders
PO Box 11608
Milwaukee, Wi 53211
414-395-2484
Feast-ed.org

18 TOOLS

In this chapter, there are three different worksheets that you can use to facilitate open communication between you and your loved one. If you are reading this as the patient, these worksheets are tools to help you communicate with your support system.

The first worksheet is for your loved one to express to you what is helpful and not helpful to them as an individual. This is a great tool to help you understand what you can do to be the best support possible.

The second worksheet is for the creative side in you, it offers two boxes, one for you to draw your interpretation of your loved one's eating disorder, as if it was a separate entity, and one for your loved one to do the same.

Discuss them when you are finished and see what is similar and what might be different.

The third worksheet is a place for your loved one to explore what their life worth living would look like. They can write, draw, compose, scribble, or rip it out, whatever works for them. When they are done with that, discuss their life worth living and see where you can help to facilitate that, and encourage them to think of what they can do to get there.

These are just tools, if they don't work for you, that is totally fine, and if they work well, make copies and revisit it every couple of months.

It can also be helpful for your loved one to read this book with a highlighter. When they find something that they relate with, they can highlight it so that you have an idea of who (and where) they are in relation to their eating disorder and in their relationship with you.

"Take what you can use, and leave the rest. It works if you work it."

~Slogan from Alcoholics Anonymous

What is Helpful Worksheet

HELPFUL	NOT HELPFUL

What is Helpful Worksheet

HELPFUL	NOT HELPFUL

What ED Looks Like

This is what MY eating disorder looks like:

What the ED Looks Like

This is what my LOVED ONE'S eating disorder looks like:

This is my LIFE WORTH LIVING!!!

My name is:

I want to reclaim these things from the eating disorder:

-
-
-

My life in one year looks like:

My life in five years looks like:

These are my three biggest dreams:

1.
2.
3.

What My Life Worth Living Looks Like

ABOUT THE AUTHOR

Haley Snyder is a graduate of the University of Minnesota – Twin Cities. Currently she has a Bachelor of Science in Psychology and is working on her Master of Arts in Clinical Psychology. She is known for her many passions which include writing, singing, and validating people who are struggling with mental illness. She has been in recovery from Anorexia since 2011 and hopes to reduce the stigma and stereotypes surrounding eating disorders by sharing her story and the wisdom that she has gained in her journey toward recovery.

CPSIA information can be obtained at www.ICGtesting.com
Printed in the USA
LVOW01s0840200914

405060LV00002B/86/P

9 781495 976919